Untangled – Ending the Culture Wars

Untangled explores one narrative that offers an explanation and a viable way forward to Untangle ourselves individually from the culture wars.

The answer to the advent of divisive and damaging theories and practices lies within the collaborative nature of individuals, and in those individuals' ability to weave a powerful narrative.

The power of storytelling is one of the most effective ways that individuals can engage and persuade others and that story should be through time, draped on facts and wisdom, and capable of changing minds.

Table of Contents

A Narrative, Not the Narrative

Oscar Wilde and his Boys

Many people associate the criminalisation of homosexuality with Oscar Wilde, but they would be mistaken, for the law that criminalised it was passed a full ten years before Oscar's trial, and acts associated with homosexuality extended as far back as 1533 and The Buggery Act (for which the penalty was death) passed by Henry the VIII.

It was the liberal politician and journalist Henry Du Pré Labouchère who raised an amendment to The Criminal Law Amendment Act 1885 that *all* homosexual acts became illegal under any circumstances, and it is into this world of born criminality that many gay men alive today knew only too well.

But that was just a small beginning, and in a way the public scandal of Oscar Wilde's spectacular fall from grace was partially responsible for raising public consciousness, even if that was only in revulsion.

Two Wars Later

In considering cultural and by default social and political events through history we may wish to be cognisant of the nature of our humanity, not least of all in the recognition that a society can be traumatised and will react if it is not led by narratives that call to our better nature.

Within a few short years post Oscar, many of them blighted by various small wars, the assassination of Archduke Franz Ferdinand plunged the us into the horror of World War 1, and British lives were altered forever.

The loss of life was extraordinary, over 880,000 in the UK alone.

A generation of men lost in the trenches and a world traumatised by conflict, for which the Industrial Revolution became the catalyst to produce war machines that had never been seen before and consequently destruction on a global scale. The subsequent passage of the Representation of the People Act of 1918 emancipated everyone, the arguments against destroyed by the bitter war that preceded it. The gradual decrepitude of the class system and moves to full enfranchisement was a sign of a progressive society.

From the comfort of our homes, we can happily watch Downton Abbey, but consider that for some alive today, they knew great grandparents and grandparents who were in service, who saw the war unfold, alongside the democratisation of the UK and the fight for rights of the disenfranchised and the birth of the Labour movement.

They were present when the whole country paused for four years, pulled together in the subsequent tough times between the wars until once again they were forced to fight for freedom as the Nazis invaded Poland.

In no less than twenty years since the Great War the UK endured the loss of another 450,000 of its citizens, and this time with a much greater civilian cost due to advances in aviation.

This time technology played a much greater part in bringing the reality of war home to the British people, the Associated British-Pathé news was born in 1933, bringing the war directly to the now affordable by all cinemas (not so in 1918) and becoming a staple of community life at the time.

The subsequent revelations of Hitler's Holocaust, (revealed at Nuremberg), and Stalin's Holodomor (hidden for years by Soviet denial) delivered a devastating blow to our collective humanity, amplified by advancing technology such as cinema, television, and the Internet, these reverberate down the generations as a warning against ideological extremism, most surely the greatest lesson to be learned from the 20th century.

This could be seen as a necessary trauma on the culture of the UK that deserves to be relived, as a warning of a century drenched in blood, replete with lessons for the future. Technology now means each generation can learn and see what depths a humanity unfettered from morality and the solid foundation of a principled populace can plumb.

The deeply normative morals of the post rationing and affluent latter half of the 1950s gave birth to the "Teenager" as a distinct category which in turn led to activism of the 1960s, much greater individual freedom and a boom in popular culture laid the template for today's world. It was obvious that the UK would never be the same again as a beleaguered cultural body began its makeover.

Born of the parental need to give children a better youth than they had had previously, the first generation free from conscription, shaped the future, and it seemed after the bleakness of the first half of the 20th century that Britain was modernising.

Hang Em High – The Traumatisation of a Nation

To some, the suspension and then abolition of the death penalty in Britain, marked that modernisation, a liberal and humanitarian leap forward that marries well with the 1960's issues of civil rights and could be seen as the starting pistol to the modern era, free from the authoritarianism of post war 50s Britain.

Occurring in 1965, this was a deeply polarising debate, but the then Labour Government passed the motion easily, despite a public outcry and the societal divisions the action caused, beginning a 5 year pause on hanging, which was finally abolished legally in 1969.

However, one event, which has left a permanent scar on the British psyche, was about to occur and traumatise a nation just 20 years from a devastating war.

In 1965 the arrest of Myra Hindley and Ian Brady and the discovery of their crimes against children fractured the social and cultural landscape. A fracture symbolised by the presence of technology in the form of audio recordings of sexual torture and murder, child abuse images that Brady had developed himself, and the photos of Myra stood at the graves of the children they had murdered.

The recordings, played in court, to a hushed audience, left scars on those who heard it and became a symbol of evil for an entire nation.

By 1959 the penetration of television into the homes of British families had reached 10,000,000, a significant figure in a population of 50,000,000 people, and provided a vivid catalyst in the public fury at the crimes of Hindley and Brady.

The revelation of Brady's and Hindley's sexual abuse and murder of boys and girls, compounded by the destruction of trust the facilitation of the female Hindley engendered, scarred the nation irrevocably and challenged many cherished ideas around woman as care giver.

When the news broke that the practices conducted by that vile duo included sexually assaulting young boys as well as girls, a few folks would have thought that worse, as if the murder and sexual assault of girls were somehow less heinous.

We should be mightily uncomfortable with that morally repugnant differentiation, just for the record.

Women were still treated like second class citizens, feminism was gaining traction, but husbands could effectively rape their wives with no penalty, right in to the 1990s, so you can bet that the revulsion was wrenched up a notch in the minds of homophobes as well as the average person, these were the morals of the time.

The Names Ian Brady and Myra Hindley became news in 1965 and have stayed in the British cultural mind to this day, with the connection between Brady being homosexual and Hindley a lesbian reported as recently as 2017 in a sickening article in the Daily Star.

Remember, being homosexual was still illegal in 1965, and although change was afoot amongst the authorities, many were unaware of the gradual move towards decriminalisation, so whether we like it or not, the absolute revulsion the public had for these terrible crimes would have, to some, been morally hierarchical, and in their minds justifiably so,

Wolfenden and Victim – A Catalyst for action

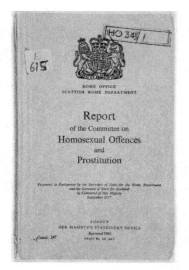

The Wolfenden report, commissioned in 1954 by Winston Churchills Government investigated the criminalisation of gay men for the first time since 1885 and the subsequent trials of Oscar Wilde. With hundreds of men being imprisoned every year, a re-examination was required, and although the matter was debated in parliament, it failed to get enough support for a change in the law to occur.

But the die had been cast, the public's understanding of homosexuality was being fed by the work of American Sexologist Alfred Kinsey in his reports that examined human sexuality in a way that had not previously occurred.

We can view this as part of the sexual revolution, casting off the shackles of the stifling conformity of the middle of the twentieth century, and the fledgling steps of embracing a new normal.

It was not an immediate change that followed but the formation of gay activist groups such as The Homosexual Law Reform Society in 1957 on the back of the inaction of the Government on the

Wolfenden report marked the first serious activism in the UK gay movement, the chink in the armour the report represented helped.

It took fully ten years after the report for the issue of decriminalising homosexuality to again enter parliamentary debate, and it was anything but progressive and enlightened, with the Labour Leader Harold Wilson against any change.

In the end it took a private members bill by Welsh politician Leo Abse to bring an end to the convoluted debate.

It won because Homosexuals should be pitied not tolerated, but as they say, any port in a storm.

The public mood was influenced once again by the media, as seen with the big events of the first half of the 20th century, and the film Victim, released in 1961 played a part in the changing of public conversation driving mass realisation that the existing law was a "Blackmailers Charter".

The presence of Dirk Bogarde, a renowned star and who was in fact himself gay, the film, directed by Basil Deardon was a successful trojan horse that was posited as a thriller. A fascinating quote from the director says a lot about the times and the lexicon of condemnation used by the public.

Sir Dirk Bogarde recalled that on the first day, Director Basil Dearden addressed the cast and crew:

"While you are here, there are to be no references to homos, poofs, queens, fags, faggots, queers, or nancy boys."

What, Bogarde asked, should they call "them"?

Dearden replied: "Inverts. That's what's in the dictionary."

In what was surely a sign of the changing times that the film went on to be nominated for two BAFTAs, for screen play and best actor for Bogarde, and garnering critical and public praise.

The similarly themed film The Children's Hour dealt with accusations of lesbianism, but as it was never a crime to be a lesbian, the film did not gain the social significance of Victim.

The Perceived Attack on the Family

It is often said that the British people are at heart centrists, we are an old country, and a fair, tolerant, and welcoming people and the film Victim did have the effect of opening debate and changing minds, the unfairness of Blackmail, often referred to as *"an attempted murder of the soul"* was a catalyst for many.

It is to this British sense of fairness and tolerance that the civil rights leaders have appealed over the years. It is no secret that the decriminalisation of homosexuality in 1967 led to a huge increase in the persecution of gay men by the police and the state, and this continued well into the eighties with James Anderton being a stark example of the level of Bigotry that the establishment gleefully wielded.

Beatrix Campbell the Journalist noted in her article of August 2004 in the Guardian

"Back then, Canal Street in Manchester city centre was still a red-light district. Anderton, an evangelical Christian, encouraged his officers to stalk its dank alleys and expose anyone caught in a clinch, while police motorboats with spotlights cruised for gay men around the canal's locks and bridges."

He was so notorious that he now holds a place in Set Four – The James Anderton Edition of Lurid Top Trumps, a fitting epitaph to a virulent bigot.

The "save the children" mantra and the protection of "family values" has been a constant companion on the road for equality in both the public, and at the time in the establishment mind. A notion of the vampiric nature in which gay men were seen to be passing on homosexuality to the young in practice and through indoctrination. This is a myth that remains in the minds of some, and the gay movement paid a heavy price for not being gatekeepers of their own movement as we shall discover.

But that British tolerance only goes so far, and the generations who have experienced trauma, and would not wish the same on their children, had their first brush with a form of neoliberalism that to this day still pops up.

PIE in 28 Sections

The formation of PIE (Paedophile Information Exchange) in 1974 brought a whole host of problems that directly stemmed from the criminalization of homosexuality and the subsequent begrudging relaxing of the law that left the age of consent at 21 for homosexuals and 16 for heterosexuals.

PIE became inexplicably linked to the gay rights movement, a wolf in sheep's clothing that meant by the time members of PIE stated they had attractions to girls as young as 8 and boys as young as 11 it was too late to extricate the nascent movement by same sex folk from it.

Again, the media went to town.

This is an example of forced teaming at its best with PIE having nothing to do with same sex attraction at all.

Today, a minor is someone under the age of 18 years according to a definition under the Births and Deaths Registration Amendment Act (No 1 of 2002). Prior to this the age of majority was 21 and reduced to 18 years by this Act. Today in law the word child is often used to describe anyone under 18.

Confusion that did nobody any favours.

It is important to realise that the language of the time that was used to describe men who had sex with any other male who was under 21, would be described as having sex with a minor, a legal term that in the minds of the public meant child. The language used today to describe the abuse of children is the same language used to denigrate gay men when an unequal age of consent existed.

This is illustrated perfectly in the case of Alan Turin, the codebreaker who worked at Bletchley Park and now rightly recognised as a hero. He was arrested in 1952 whilst in the University of Manchester for having an affair with a 19-year-old, he was found dead 2 years later after attempts to chemically convert his same sex attraction by injecting him with synthetic Oestrogen which caused him to grow breasts.

These cases provided mana from heaven to the salacious media, but more importantly allowed for the obfuscation in public language and culture of what would now be seen as a consenting individual at 16, but then as a child unable to consent even if 20.

A headline, article or for that matter a chat in the local pub, prior to the age of consent being lowered for gay men to 18 in 2000, could have posited gay men as sexually assaulting that child of 20. A situation that would not have existed if equalisation had been immediate with the 1967 act, or better still if being gay had never been a crime at all!

Into this breach stepped PIE, and in the progressive and free rolling civil rights movements of the 70's they gained some sway, even being feted by other gay groups, the Left of the Labour Party, Liberty and the likes of Harriet Harman and Patricia Hewitt.

Yes, they were vastly contrasting times indeed, and it took a while before the gay movement could extricate itself from the mess and the public opprobrium that followed. The memory of PIE loomed large in the public mind for many years, and it was not until 2006 the existence of PIE was finally ended, and its members brought to justice.

The Gift to the Homophobes

As if the turmoil of the previous twenty years were not enough for the gay community when equality was just a distant desire, mother nature landed them with an atrocity that would forever change the world and almost wipe a generation of gay men from the planet. Just 16 years from decriminalisation in 1964 the AIDS crisis began.

The CDC (Centre for Disease Control) in the USA provides an excellent timeline of events from the American perspective whilst the Independent filled in the gaps for the UK in the wake of the syrupy and inaccurate C4 Drama It's a Sin.

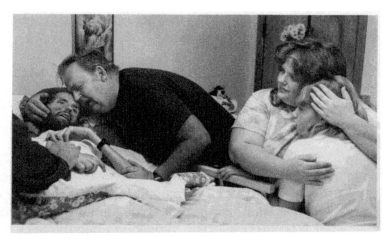

The first cases of GRID (Gay Related Immune Deficiency Syndrome) as it was originally known, and what we now call HIV/AIDS came to the public consciousness in California and New York City. The story surrounding the discovery is covered brilliantly in the novel And the Band Played On: Politics, People, and the AIDS Epidemic by Randy Schultz and summarised well in the HBO film of the same name from 1993.

It is hard to describe the fear, disgust and hate that ripped through the population of the UK in the wake of the AIDS crisis, and it was not until 1987 that the public health campaign kicked into high gear (with the now infamous Iceberg advert) that this was seen as anything other than the *"Anally Injected Death Sentence"* that homophobes loved to shout at gay men alongside the ever present slur "Queer".

For an already beleaguered community this was devastating, and for moral demagogues promulgating their own anti-gay agenda the homophobia in the UK reached new heights of ferocity. The stories of abandonment and cruelty were mirrored in countries all over the globe, the new untouchables had arrived, and the world would never be the same again.

The media rolled out an anti-fact, anti-science, and wholly western narrative (it was not a gay plague in Africa for a start, it got anyone it could) offered up, as a brief, convenient and comforting lie to the heterosexual population, who, if they had been the first victims, would have seen a rosier and swifter response from the authorities, on that you can bet.

People in the West, going about their daily lives simply did not know better, no Internet, no Facebook, no anything except the old-fashioned media, newspapers, and a few TV channels, this is not the media landscape today.

To expect that Barbara and Ahmed, getting the kids ready for school, would have a reason to, or even knew they should try, fostering understanding and compassion to gay folk, is surely incredibly naïve?

This rarely happened even when people were directly connected to a gay person by blood or friendship, abandonment was the order of the day, especially in the culture storm that was busily lying about the science and the reality.

Fuelled by anti-homosexual propaganda, both historic and recent, from the church, establishment, and media, this was, and still is in some areas now, an impossible ask for the Barbara's and Ahmed's of today, an ask that that some minorities could do well to consider as they push the boundaries of our shared cultural morality.

The Incremental Sex Lives of the Gays

We are forced to recognise that progress is not always up, or in the direction of a perceived liberal world view that has dominated the UK since the 60's. Impediments exist, a change in law is not an end, it is the beginning, for public tolerance is a far greater nut to crack, ask any minority.

The hurdles the public had to jump in this race for a liberal and tolerant future were not easy, war, the end of the death sentence, the horrors of the crimes of Hindley and Brady, PIE, the AIDS crisis, and the constant fear mongering of the media left us with a nation that could be described as traumatised.

It does not take Einstein to see that the population of the UK may well have not been ready for schoolchildren to learn about same sex attraction. To an uneducated populace when it came to AIDS and gay people what did activists think (although they did not think at all it seems) was going to happen when the book "Jenny lives with Eric and Martin" appeared in schools and had the temerity to normalise gay relationships and tell children it was OK to be gay?

The media backlash was swift, "Homosexual Propaganda" became the new buzz word and poured petrol on the existing precarious position of same sex attracted people often seen as spreaders of disease and "Pervert Queers" who gave succour to paedophiles from PIE.

The press then gleefully presented it to the public, devoid of any context, and riven with every panic and concern that had occurred in the past 40 years, indelibly etched on our cultural psyche.

This led to the passing of legislation that became known as Section 28, a pernicious amendment that banned the promotion of Homosexuality in schools.

Status: This is the original version (as it was originally enacted).

28   Prohibition on promoting homosexuality by teaching or by publishing material

(1)   The following section shall be inserted after section 2 of the [1986 c. 10.] Local Government Act 1986 (prohibition of political publicity):—

"2A   Prohibition on promoting homosexuality by teaching or by publishing material

(1)   A local authority shall not—

     (a)   intentionally promote homosexuality or publish material with the intention of promoting homosexuality;

     (b)   promote the teaching in any maintained school of the acceptability of homosexuality as a pretended family relationship.

(2)   Nothing in subsection (1) above shall be taken to prohibit the doing of anything for the purpose of treating or preventing the spread of disease.

(3)   In any proceedings in connection with the application of this section a court shall draw such inferences as to the intention of the local authority as may reasonably be drawn from the evidence before it.

(4)   In subsection (1)(b) above 'maintained school' means,—

     (a)   in England and Wales, a county school, voluntary school, nursery school or special school, within the meaning of the Education Act 1944, and

     (b)   in Scotland, a public school, nursery school or special school, within the meaning of the Education (Scotland) Act 1980."

(2)   This section shall come into force at the end of the period of two months beginning with the day on which this Act is passed.

The effect on some people was real, as can be seen in this item, but there is also a mass of misinformation about this legislation, and when examples of its actual use in law are asked for, they never appear because it never was used.

Section 28 was a reactive piece of legislation, which illustrates that when progressive forces are unable to recognise and clearly delineate the cultural zeitgeist of the times, they are likely to overstep the mark.

Because Section 28 proved popular to a vastly different public than today, prompted by historical prejudice and misunderstanding, the current fear of AIDS and the activities of PIE, when Thatcher stated *"...they have an inalienable right to be gay..."*, many agreed that was not on, at least not yet...

That enough condemns her in most people's minds, but we are forced to recognise the cultural reality of Britain at the time, that the idea that the gays were after the kids was a palpably sellable one for political gain, and an equally easy one to buy for the public.

"Made it, Ma! Top of the world!"

There may be a naivety in imagining the Thatcher Government, in the turmoil of the prehistory and the reality of the 1980s had carte blanche to give gay people all the equality we now enjoy, as if that vista would have even been open to her if she had wanted to (which I doubt), is astoundingly innocent of the nature of Statehood and cultural and social change.

At that time, in the eyes of many, the attitude held sway that "the gays" were gleefully killing each other through their sexual promiscuity by" choosing" the original (illegal) sin of being homosexual in the first place, an idea that has recently resurfaced.

Despite words many heard far too many times, which scarred them emotionally as an individual, "they deserve what they get," or in one disgusting case of an AIDS sufferer, "...he was 17, he was a criminal, that's natural justice...", I am bound to set aside valid but unhealthy emotion and consider the following.

Is it possible, in the febrile atmosphere that existed, where homosexuality was begrudgingly tolerated by some and hated by the many, a nuanced approach to change was required, because if it was the actual desire of the authorities at the time to criminalise same sex attraction completely once more, the public support may well have been with them?

Considering that in 1967, Lady Thatcher voted in favour of the decriminalisation of homosexuality, in the face of fierce opposition from Tory traditionalists, we may want to question why she supported Section 28, and I imagine it requires more nuanced reasoning than contemporary understanding.

Could it be that enlightened folk, lovers of freedom, were fighting with all their might against authoritarian forces, both right and left? Protecting children may well have been what section 28 was about, but from whom?

In the eyes of many in the public sphere, child molesters and perverts and unpopular as it may be, the failure to deal with PIE and other extremists led to the law existing, and responsibility for that awful situation is not with hindsight so easily distributed.

The little book that started this is harmless by today's standards to rational folk, certainly it is nowhere near as troublesome as what is being taught to children today in the name of "Gender Identity Ideology and Queer theory."

Same sex attracted folks now enjoy full protection under the law, the change was incremental and could have been better, but these days we are done, and that is worth celebrating, we have indeed made it.

We are 12 years from the Equality Act 2010, and we are nowhere near living up to the standards that signifies, but it is fair to say that it is in Disability rights that we are in need of improvement, and with new rights battles on the horizon, women and same sex attracted folk are once again having to battle for their existing rights, and this time against those who they have supported so fervently in times gone by.

"Made it, Ma! Top of the world!

Well, not just yet.

The Not So Dim and Distant Past
In the 1940's and into the 50's Britain was still reeling from the second world war, rationing, the death of a vast number of young men, and loved ones who died at home during the bombings, Britain was a bruised and battered country.

One that could not be anything else but resolute in the need to construct a new Britain, a healing Britain, and that is exactly what they did.

The post war Labour Government of 1945 passed a series of measures which became known as the 'Welfare State'. These reforms were designed to take care of the British people 'from the cradle to the grave'.

That phrase has remained in the psyche of our collective mind, a historic echo of the fortitude and resolve of those known as the "Greatest Generation."

The NHS, ungainly behemoth that it can be, is a direct result of that and it also gave us the social net that exists to help folk when unemployed, alongside a myriad of other things that opened the gate for such important movements as the autonomy and dignity of the disabled.

The Alan Turin scandal brought a new character for denigration to the public, and the fact that he was reporting a crime of theft to the police when they used that as an excuse for the state to hound him to his death would have meant little to the public, Homosexuality was the crime of the day.

The end of the death sentence in the UK, the Moors Murders, a few years later the case of Mary Bell, a child killer and then the horrific reign of Peter Sutcliffe the Yorkshire Ripper from 1975 to 1980.

There are of course more seismic events in the public sphere such as these, for they shaped opinion, through media, and through discourse and 20 today, then it will have influenced the thinking of your parents and most definitely your grandparents.

It really is not that long ago, so consider that the law decriminalised homosexuality in 1967, 22 years after World War II, the equalising of the age of consent came in 2000 33 years and many blighted lives later.

We are now 22 years from 2000, 53 years from 1967 and 75 years from WWII, and from a statesmanship point of view that is a blink in time.

Looking back in this way reduces the sense of that time and we can easily understand how the culture, fears, misunderstandings of history, societal scars of loss and societal joys at a win are embedded in that historical cultural and societal narrative landscape.

The stories told, infused with emotionality, honed by rational and critical thought, fractured by the human frailty of true remembrance can and have been exchanged through just three people, your Grandad told your Mum who told you, and that repeats back though time.

A kind of time travel, an ability to survey the receding historical horizon and learn from and share its hidden and often only retrospectively viewable meaning.

This opens the opportunity to reflect, that your great grandparents interpreted these experiences in a context underpinned by wars and the loss of millions of lives as well as having the crushing, shared human guilt over the joint atrocities of the Holocaust and the Holodomor.

All these extraordinary events would have been laid over a cultural landscape with an established moral order that came directly from Victorian England, the Oscar Wilde trial, and the criminalization of gay men.

The Selling of Fear and Panic

Satan in the Suburbs

The publishing of a faked memoir called Michelle Remembers in 1980, which became a seminal influencer in the teaching of Social Work, was a phenomenon that lit the blue touch paper on the child abuse panics that set the western world alight for many years.

In California in 1983 a distraught mother reported to the police that her pre-school child had been sodomized by Ray Buckey, the grandson of Peggy Bucky who had founded the McMartin Pre-school some years previously.

This set-in motion a chain of events that led to the longest trial in American history into alleged child abuse.

What was not known at the time was that this would spark a moral panic and spread from America to the UK, where social workers and police were trained in methodologies that would prove devastating for many children and their families.

By 1984 huge sums of money were spent on "rooting out" perceived satanic cults and cabals of people systematically abusing children.

Once again, the unreasoning moral entrepreneurs had found a new cause.

The trial itself lasted 7 years, nobody was convicted, and the procedures used by both the police (trawling for allegations) and the social services (coercive questioning, shaming and dodgy medical examinations) meant that before the discovery of the damaged caused was revealed, many years had passed.

The interviews of the children, managed by Kee McFarlane, a believer in the Satanic Child Abuse Myths and whose discredited techniques have informed child abuse investigations to this day, showed evidence of coercion and leading questions.

As one of the children said themselves once in adulthood...

> "Never did anyone do anything to me, and I never saw them doing anything. I said a lot of things that didn't happen. I lied. ... Anytime I would give them an answer that they didn't like, they would ask again and encourage me to give them the answer they were looking for. ... I felt uncomfortable and a little ashamed that I was being dishonest. But at the same time, being the type of person I was, whatever my parents wanted me to do, I would do."

The Ideological Derangement of Social Work

This corrupt template was exported to the UK and the lengthy period of the USA trial meant that these ideas took hold and became practice, feeding the overzealous long before they underwent the careful evidence-based evaluation required.

By 1987 children and their parents had fallen foul of these practices, and assertions were made that led to a government enquiry set up in the wake of the cases in Teesside where 121 children were identified and subsequently many removed form their parental homes to be fostered out.

By 1988 Judge Elizabeth Butler-Sloss had released a report commissioned by the government and which led directly to the Children's Act of 1988.

Nevertheless, in 1991 the Orkney case broke, and the Judge at the time...

"...criticised the social workers involved, saying that their handling of the case had been "fundamentally flawed," and he found in summary that "these proceedings are so fatally flawed as to be incompetent" and that the children concerned had been separated and subjected to repeated cross-examinations almost as if the aim was to force confessions rather than to assist in therapy."

The shadow of McMartin and the practices developed still in existence some 10 years later.

This was just two of the highly publicised instances in the UK, but the combined effect of these cases; as well as the abuses by religious orders and the record of brutality in children's homes, traumatised the populace once more, again with the protection of children, a vital endeavour, being at the root of not just best practice, but also worst practice, an indicator of our basic humanity surely?

Those Nasty Videos

Enter stage left the advent of home video, and with it a new and exciting item in the arsenal of the moral entrepreneurs.

Britain was a heavily censorious country at the best of times, so the idea that people in their own homes could watch whatever they wanted and whenever filled the likes of David Bright MP with horror. He gathered the worst he could find and edited them into a highlight reel that he showed to other MPs, totally devoid of context.

We were off and running in no time, and a list was drawn up of those films that should be banned, which if course provided a list to the public of those that must be watched, bringing films that were so without merit a status that they did not deserve.

These various cheap and tacky productions included a supposedly horrific scene of brutal torture by rats in "The Beast in Heat", a ridiculously low budget Nazi romp, in which the camera pans slowly around to reveal the naked woman (no surprise on that one) covered in blood and writhing in agony, whilst two disgruntled fluffy guinea pigs, who have endured the ignominy of being dyed black, sit on her body.

The panic was started and the call for more censorship went out once again and a bill was drawn up. So extreme was this legislation it was only realised at the last minute that it would effectively ban films such as the Godfather and Apocalypse now.

The bill was passed as the Video Recording Act 1984, and it ushered in an era of censorship which also handed great power to the quango the BBFC. For a time, classics such as The Exorcist and The Texas Chainsaw Massacre were unavailable to the public, effectively banned by James Ferman the draconian chief censor.

The Video Nasties Scare as it became known, again had moralists who used parental fears as a tool for political gains, but in doing so, succeeded in canonising some dreadful films forever in the memory of the public.

This tool for power and the creation of fear and panic was used again to exacerbate and trivialise the murder of James Bulger in 1993, a further scar on the psyche of the UK, a horrific reminder to us all that even children can commit wicked acts. Accusation that the killers were inspired by "Childs Play" 1988 (an innocuous horror film) arose, despite no evidence of them ever having watched it being in existence. This led James Ferman to ban "Natural Born Killers" 1994 in the UK for no reason whatsoever, a film that ironically condemned the media for the glorification of real violence.

It appears, and maybe to nobody's surprise, that moral panics lead to knee jerk reactions.

The Strangled Freedoms of the Vulnerable Child

It should come as no surprise, that the febrile atmosphere of fear surrounding the UK and particularly the safety of children cemented a generational divide, particularly between children and people who are non-familial, and that still exists today, not as the main driver, but as one of many, with technology playing a huge part.

For a period, protectionism ran amok, the term Helicopter Parenting has now been placed in the dictionary, as a phenomenon first posited in the late 60's it has become the default for many parents.

This, and the growing recognition that we may have coddled our children to such an extent we have made them weak, is going to be one of the big challenges of the next few years. Much of the evidence for this is anecdotal, it has been seen manifesting in several ways as people enter adulthood, in particular the workplace and/or higher education where some seem incapable of adult behaviour.

They call for trigger warnings, safe spaces, restrictions on speech as "actual violence" as well as displaying wholesale capitulation to ridiculous belief systems such as Postmodernism, Queer Theory and Gender Ideology and in some cases murderous Communism. This over protection, no matter from where it manifested, has had effect, and its worst manifestation; the call to "Victimhood" is probably the most dangerous.

This is because in the now therapeutic culture (post the death of Princess Diana and the hyper emotionalisation of the public sphere) we have developed in the UK, to be victim is to be saintly. Jonathan Heidt and Gregg Lukianoff caution against this phenomenon in the book The Coddling of the American Mind and Frank Furedi warned over 20 years ago of what we are seeing now in Therapy Cultures, as therapeutics are sold like burgers and weakness is celebrated and encouraged often as Victim Tribalism, particularly around immutable characteristics defined by the Equality Act.

This has the perverse effect of pitting groups against each other as various rights claims come to the fore, sowing division, confusion and in some cases provoking violence.

These states of fear and victimhood that are generated in the media drenched landscape of everyday life will come with a price, for this is a crisis, a very real one, where we have swapped exploration for fear and exchanged growth for narcissistic navel gazing.

The Uneducated Educated

The Loss of Shared Narratives and the Great "Queering"

The works of philosophers and activists from France and the USA have birthed a monstrous progeny which a gullible and forlorn educational establishment, bruised by the fall of communism and the dispersal of the Marxist dream, grabbed with both hands. The publishing of the Postmodern Condition in 1979 was pivotal.

From moderate lefty lovelies to Marxists through to full blown Communists the ideological fiats of the extreme left have dominated education for over 60 years. In that time, they have carried out various new-fangled practices and theories, some good, some bad and some downright awful, in their never-ending quest for the utopian method. This is deliberately encouraged by the disgruntled academic left and has been for many years. Hence some awfully nice people who are doing some awful things, alongside some truly awful people hell bent on doing some truly awful things.

In training the next generation of educators, academia has gone by the principle that education should be political, and the goal should be activism (Critical Pedagogy). These theories, born of the humanities between the 1960s and 1990s are generally in the business of complicating the simplistic and simplifying the complicated. They espouse an abandonment of objective in place of the subjective and exist purely to disrupt, wherever they can, using a template for activism that relies on identity politics, division, and distrust. This is termed "The Long March Through the Institutions"

What occurs in Academia eventually filters down to the rest of us, that is why academics are afforded not only public monies, but also public trust. A trust they are in danger of imminently losing.

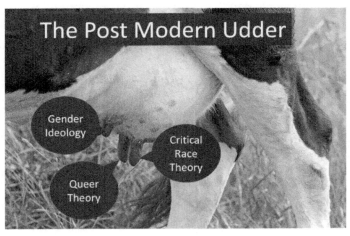

The theories espoused are anti-science, anti-enlightenment, and anti-human. Technology, the proliferation of information and the abandonment of critical thought for emotionality (a direct result of infantilising people via the protection of the child) have allowed them unprecedented and unchallenged success. A deeper examination of Gender Ideology, Queer theory and Critical Race Theory can be fruitful but is beyond this small book.

It is not hard to understand how ideologies have creeped into the educational institutions of the nation, this totalitarian American political undertaking has taken years. It is now blossoming as the lines between professional, political, and personal breakdown and our digital lives intersect those three domains, it is affecting us all.

The decision of Tony Blair and his Government in 1999 to get 50% of the population into university may have been borne of good intentions, but it could also be seen as a mistake. The proliferation of certain degrees (that have little rigour let alone any grounding, other than the fair-weather thoughts Ideologues had fed into them in a never-ending academic circle jerk of self-referencing and recapitulation) are causing this ideological crisis in education.

Students, raised in the oxygen of over protection are set awash on the shores of institutions, which push the very infantilising and victimhood narrative by which they were already hamstrung. They bought many of the Tenets the new orthodoxy espoused and in time went on to become HR bureaucrats, administrators, and teachers.

Teachers were, it seems, particularly susceptible to these new theories of weakness, grievance, power and oppression and the twinned anti-human narratives.

A Template of Tyranny and Grievance

Enter the worst of the educational theories, the scourge of Critical Pedagogy (the approach to teaching), a noxious and universal template for political activism whose adherents can apply it to; and therefore, infect any teaching endeavour, is now in full swing.

The fact that if it "ain't broke do not fix it" never enters their minds, (for narcissistic self-aggrandisement is a pre-requisite for utopianism) is a blind spot that will leave many good-hearted folks oblivious to the fact that they are the bad guys.

Even the name "Critical Pedagogy" is a misnomer, it has little to do with the approach to teaching, for it is fleetingly interested in sharing knowledge, but obsessed with critiquing existing knowledge, through a Critical Social Justice lens, peering Sauron like over every discipline for stories of power and oppression.

It is to all intents and purposes a parasitical ideology that calls for a power and oppression lens of Critical Social Justice to be used as the tool for creating the next wave of activists, filled with deranged enragement by histories they can never change and eager to fight battles already won.

It is indoctrination, not education, for the seed from which it springs is inculcated on superiority and smacks of a back seat driver Maiden Aunt.

This is the price of this "parental" approach to education, for the generations of CSJ (Critical Social Justice) devotees who say lots; but do little, will become the leaders of tomorrow, as children, in adult bodies.

In form it is profoundly nannying and deeply authoritarian, like the mummy and daddy nobody would wish for.

In no time at all new waves of activists left school, headed to university, and subsequently became the next generation of activists, ready and waiting for the right moment, and then that moment came.

On the 25th of May 2020 George Floyd died in America, and his death triggered protests around the world. And academia lost its collective mind.

Tens of thousands of academics signed up to activities such as #shutdownstem without even knowing what they were signing was a hoax from 4chan.

Universities began recommending a plethora of books written by left wing extremists without thinking for a second what they were doing, and we were off and running. Driven, by the false idea that students are the customers they must please and blind to the fact they are not the customer, society is, the student is the product. People supported the extremist organisation BLM without a thought to the dangerous ideology they push.

At the time critical thought seemed to have taken a holiday.

The Curation of a Feared Existence

We are in a crisis, a crisis of education, and there is not one institution that can do anything about it. This crisis is personal, only fixable by the individual and many of us do not even know the crisis exists. This crisis is not going anywhere fast, we are, put simply, drowning, and starving.

It is a form of drowning that does not deprive the individual of oxygen, but of personal space, and the starvation is one of meaning. This is an intellectual crisis, a knowledge crisis, and the driver is information.

We are a species assailed, mostly with nonsense, from the second we pick up a smart phone in the am, to the minute we turn of whatever device has our attention last thing at night. Not all of us, quite obviously, but a huge proportion, and this is how many of our lives are now experienced in a nutshell.

No wonder then, when we consider the plethora of messages that we receive throughout the day, we have defaulted to a simplistic and infant like capacity to categorise over examine. To default, with an inevitable but unfelt exhaustion, to skimming headlines; and other information, just long enough for us to guess (for it is only a guess in the deluge) it either upsets us or makes us feel better, enrages, or calms us, catches us through the novelty of the new or bores us with the dullness of familiarity.

In the end it may not matter, as our tiny minds capitulate to the huge influx of information, descending in a spiral of camouflaged decisions like those described above, we resort to the infantile "good" or "bad" as we confine what we see either to oblivion; or a cursory glance and the intention of "I will read that later."

A later that never comes.

The camouflaged behaviour is powerful, we may think that we are making a choice of free will, but are in fact practicing free won't, in the deep human need to find patterns and discern sense from the mostly nonsensical and meaning from the largely meaningless.

Beset with personalised levels of rubbish from the algorithms that dictate what you see, and by default who sees what you create, we find ourselves in a profoundly behaviourist environment. But not necessarily in the human need to educate, but in an unfettered global classroom where little thought is given to the individual and indoctrination, dehumanising and cultish responses are the norm.

Where the interactions of everyday are conducted by an invisible parental figure, a dystopian Wizard of Oz, hidden behind the curtain of impenetrable information. This is frightening, as the path we currently take is steeped in groupings, political and private, identity driven, and demanding, from crackpot activists to paraphiliac fetishists.

Segregation Forever

At the same time, the lines between the personal sphere, the private sphere and the personal self and private self are looking decidedly blurred if not disappearing altogether.

Bring your whole self to work, be the real you, become your authentic self are the slogans of choice and the mantras of the day, marketed as an absolute good when they are anything but. The ephemera of PR, branding and marketing as social good, the trojan horses of control, capitulation, and performance.

This is a ticking time bomb for misunderstanding, mental derangement, and conflict.

It is hardly surprising, as the often cited, and wildly misunderstood mantra of 70s feminism, "The Personal is Political" seems to have become flesh for all of us, far removed from its original meaning and intent. It is this misunderstanding we need an antidote for, as the statement as long since been hijacked.

Despite calls for further entrenchment of this view, as in the confusing article by Gila Stopler *"The personal is political: The feminist critique of liberalism and the challenge of right-wing populism,"* which seems to blame not recognising the truth of the statement did lead to a backlash from the far right, we should consider that the absolute opposite is required.

It also posits that what is now needed is more of its application not less, and in doing so the writer argues for a creepy and deeply behavioural interference in people's private lives. In a world where the individual is assailed by "bullshit" to put it plainly, there has never been a greater need to develop a personal persona capable of deep understanding and critical thinking.

Unflustered by the desperately needed low altitude, high resolution critical thinking and cognisant of the need for meaty deep learning alongside the chewing gum for the brain everyday life has become. A persona that eschews the external branding of virtue signalling gullibility and group membership ritualism in return for an inner development driven by responsibility, a sense of your own morality, the creation and solidifying of meaning.

This developmental need so many crave, but do not have the tools to excavate, is a crisis that will become more constrictive. It will blunt our lives and render us as the comatose progeny of an over weaning and uncaring parental figure from whom we cannot escape, but whose control we so desperately covet in a world where we are constantly assaulted by the presence of others.

We must rebuild the personal private space, and in doing so, create societies that treasure it and protect it, for as always, the greatest threat to humanity is each other, and the fragmentation of historically tenacious spaces helps nobody.

We need to segregate, and we need to do it fast, before all our lives become curated fodder for the miasma of cyberspace. The segregation to selfhood and thought. This human need to want to be better, more educated, more erudite, more tolerable, more social, and just maybe ...more complete, should not be at the whim of technology or an over weaning parent.

We should worry more about our growth as individuals, a growth that may reveal what you can do to enrich yours and others lives and is less about the introspective emotionalised outward project of branding, fake personae creation and the affirmation of the given mob.

In a world assailed by mere information, the search for and propagation of knowledge becomes a right of all individuals, but also a responsibility, and one we should take seriously and consider deeply.

For in this world, we all become teachers and we all become pupils.

Get this right and with a little luck, the crisis in education, and our societies taste for the easy and unreal, will subside.

So how can we see a way to untangle this mess?

Consider what follows...

Planting a New Seed – We are Both Pupils and Teachers

Despite a bloat of theoretical activity in the educational academic sphere, when you boil it down, any educational endeavour will begin with a simple binary choice, a choice between two seeds, yes, it is that simple.

The first "seed" flourishes on the belief that the individual must be nudged, manipulated, and coerced covertly to the educational objective. The second "seed" sees the individual is capable of autonomy, aided and resourced they will learn themselves?

Both are vital, some will say, and they are correct that in cooperation, teachers use these methods the world over. However, what we are looking at here is not the how of teaching (methodology), but the foundational why (philosophy), that underpins practice in the field.

We are talking philosophical not methodological. The first seed, implies what is known as a "Behaviourist Orientation" (Pavlov's Dogs) to teaching, whilst the second a "Humanist Approach" (Self exploration). But what will be the foundational idea (orientation to) behind the teaching in this new existence?

Which seed will you choose, the first or second?

For you can only plant one seed, so choose wisely, for in the cognitively complex world we inhabit and are destined for we all become teachers, we all become pupils, so which is it to be?

The second seed, simply put, is the belief that individuals are capable of learning and making decisions themselves based on that learning, classically liberal if you will and confirmed in the beliefs of enlightenment values...

Critical Pedagogy lies in the first "seed," a part of the behaviourist orientation with little regard for the individual who can be "nudged" and "covertly coerced" at the political whims of the ideologue before them, who insists on adherence to the given template, not an individual's understanding of the wider landscape.

The Curriculum of Identitarianism

They often do this in the name of Equality, Diversity, and Inclusion (EDI), (a mess of an Industry, birthed in the fight for civil liberties and fuelled by the Equality Act 2010) and in doing so they become the literal wolf in sheep's clothing, for this is not a call for equality that respects the individual, diversity of thought and collaborative inclusion, it is exactly the opposite, it is the power and oppression narratives of the disgruntled and mediocre.

The equality they espouse is based upon a philosophy that is behaviourist, which assumes that the individual is not autonomous and capable. But only valid as part of a group. This is their philosophical anchor to any learning, their default position from which methodology grows.

Their foundation is built on a hierarchical inequality that posits the teacher as the holder of "a truth" that can be used to manipulate (not enlighten) the learner in whichever ideological way they choose. That is not equality, that is inequality, from the very outset.

The diversity they call for is steeped in identity politics, for teaching is political to them, and group identity trumps individualism. That is not diversity, that is homogenised discrimination, which excludes the unbeliever, the wrong kind of Gay, the wrong kind of Woman, wrong kind of Black.

By inclusion they mean adherence to the dogmatic nature of their theories. That is not inclusion, for the identity politics requires the ingroup, an individual unbeliever will be in the outgroup, nothing inclusive about that. They require compliance and not thought, the new mantras and tenets of "Critical Social Justice Teaching" are creating in people an inner wasteland, devoid of individual analysis and exploration, they are creating drone like activists' hell bent on collective disruption and not collaboration.

In using this moribund and anti-human philosophy of activism, they effectively quell equality unless you are part of a group, eschew diversity that is not ascribed by shared characteristics and make wretched the idea of collaborative inclusivity for selected collectivist naval gazing.

The individuals who succumb to using this template of grievance may well regret it as the reality of life bites and bites hard. For to espouse group identitarian mantras is to lose the self, to become a walking billboard for grievance and an advertisement for the worst elements of tribalism.

These profoundly depressing activities taking place are driven by extremists that may not even know they are the bad guys, for it has not occurred to them, nor will it whilst people sit silently by and let it happen, betraying a need to understand a world that is effectively now a classroom filled with information.

The Horseshoe of Extremism

A conundrum of this divisive political phenomenon is that we are mostly adept at seeing when the political right goes too far, for obvious reasons, yet are not as good at defining when the political left is doing the same.

Perhaps we are seeing the answer emerge in the distinct difference of philosophical orientation that they both share, the Pavlov's dogs' approach to other humans, the behaviourist orientation, with humans as creatures to manipulate and use in the "ends justify the means" minds of Utopian Ideologues of all political hues. For they share the same seed, but as the seed germinates, the dichotomy of the first two leaves is the same in devastating outcome, but vastly different in philosophically wicked essence.

The far right think their detractors are lesser than them, leading them to the murderous instinct to kill.

The left believe that they are better than their detractors and will kill them with utopian and collectivist driven kindness.

The Holodomor meets the Holocaust.

Or, if you will, the right is violent masculinity, and the left is violent femininity, take your pick.

These toxic manifestations of the human spirit have nothing to do with being a man or a woman, the starting place of our civilisation, knowing who and what we are. They are the opposite of the grand ideas that we are all autonomous individuals with the capacity to learn and the fact that education is profoundly humanist in nature.

The ideologues would have you believe otherwise, and the more we can spot them the more we can call them out, and maybe, just maybe, undo the harm done by the far left to some of our most trusted institutions.

Perhaps then we can go some way to using our basic humanity to warn against and help us all avoid the machinations of fear mongers and ideologues of every hue.

The clear message is...

"We are not Pavlov's Dogs."

Printed in Great Britain
by Amazon

42472391R00020